TM

THE BOOK AND CD ~~~~~ORK TOGETHER

T0124099

VIKINGS

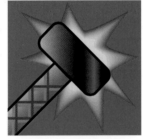

TWO CAN TM

PRINCETON ■ LONDON

www.two-canpublishing.com

Published in the United States and Canada by
Two-Can Publishing LLC, 234 Nassau Street, Princeton, NJ 08542

© 2001, 1997 Two-Can Publishing
Book text © Robert Nicholson

For information on Two-Can books and multimedia,
call 1-609-921-6700, fax 1-609-921-3349, or visit our Web site at
http://www.two-canpublishing.com

CD
Creative Director: Jason Page
Programming Director: Brett Cropley
Art Director: Sarah Evans
Senior Designer: James Evans
Sub Editor: Jo Keane
Consultant: Tim Wood
Illustrators: James Jarvis, Carlo Tartaglia, Jeffrey Lewis,
John Richardson, Dai Owen
Production Manager: Joya Bart-Plange

Book
Creative Director: Jason Page
Editors: Kate Graham, Jo Keane, Alison Woodhouse
Authors: Robert Nicholson and Claire Watts
Consultant: Tim Wood
Art Director: Belinda Webster
Designer: Michele Egar
Production Manager: Joya Bart-Plange

Created by
act-two
346 Old Street, London EC1V 9RB

ISBN 1-58728-467-7

2 3 4 5 6 7 8 9 10 02

Photograph Credits: front cover Werner Forman Archives
p.10, p.11, p.12, p.13, p.14, p.15, p.16, p.17, p.20, p.21, p.24 t, p.25, p.27, p.34 t, p.36 b Werner
Forman; p.24 b, p.26 Toby Maudsley; p.34 c Ronald Sheridan; p.23, p.28 York Archaeological Trust.
Illustrations: p. 6–7, p.13, p.15, pp.16–17, p.18, p.21, pp.22–23, pp.26–27,
p.28 Kevin Maddison; pp.29–33 Maxine Hamil

Printed in Hong Kong by Wing King Tong

INTERFACT

THE BOOK AND CD THAT WORK TOGETHER

INTERFACT will have you hooked in minutes – and that's a fact!

⬤ **The disk is packed with interactive activities, puzzles, quizzes, and games that are fun to do and packed with interesting facts.**

Explore a Viking village on screen and learn how the Vikings lived.

Food

Food was an important part of the Vikings' life. Very little land was fertile, and the winters were long and harsh. The Vikings ate fish and stews of beef or lamb. They grew vegetables such as peas, cabbage, beans, wild leeks, and garlic.

Tables were set up for meals, and family members would sit on the same wooden benches that they slept on at night. They ate from rectangular wooden platters or soapstone bowls, using spoons and knives that they carried on their belts.

The Vikings used drinking horns as well as cups. The horns did not have flat bottoms, so they were passed around the table until they were empty. A man who could empty a drinking horn in one turn was admired. The usual drink was mead, a sweet beer made from honey.

Food facts

● The Vikings used peas to make bread when they had no grain.
● They got salt by boiling sea water.
● The Vikings ate two meals a day: the day meal after the early farm work and the night meal at the end of the day.

▼ Vikings cooked over an open hearth fire. They roasted meat on huge spits and made stews in big iron caldrons. Sometimes they used a gridiron made of coiled iron, below. They heated it in a fire then placed it underneath a cooking pot. Does it remind you of part of a modern stove?

▼ Bowls were made from pottery or soapstone.

These Vikings are having a meal. To find out more about the Vikings' eating habits click here.

Click to continue

⬤ **Open the book and discover more fascinating information, highlighted with lots of full-color illustrations and photographs.**

Read about what the Vikings ate and how they cooked their food.

⬤ To get the most out of **INTERFACT**, use the book and disk together. Watch for the special signs, called Disk Links and Bookmarks. To find out more, turn to page 43.

23

BOOKMARK

DISK LINK
Would you like to play a Viking board game? Try hnefatafl!

Once you've launched **INTERFACT** you'll never look back.

LOAD UP!
Go to **page 40** to find out how to load your disks and click into action.

3

HELP SCREEN

Learn how to use the disk in no time at all.

Welcome to the

INTERFACT

disk on Vikings

To have a look at all the different things on the disk, simply click the arrow keys with your mouse.

As you do this, you'll see a description of each activity in the reading box.

Click on the picture at the top of the screen to select the activity you want to investigate.

These are the controls the Help Screen will tell you how to use:
- arrow keys
- reading boxes
- 'hot' words

DAN THE DANE

Did the Vikings just raid and pillage? What were they really like?

Let Dan the Dane answer all your questions about the Viking warriors and learn all you need to know about their weapons, tactics, raids, and settlements.

RUNE WRITING

Learn about the Viking alphabet and write your own message in runes.

Type a message in runes and discover the sound that each symbol represents. Click your mouse on the Viking to learn the history of the futhark alphabet.

VIKING VILLAGE

Explore a typical Viking village. There's lots for you to see!

You can check out:
- what's on the menu for dinner
- why Viking houses were smelly
- what the Vikings did for fun

WALLOP!

Do you think you've got what it takes to be a true Vikings expert?

Test your brain power with this fact-filled quiz. But watch out. Thor, the god of thunder, will bonk you with his hammer if you blunder. So, brush up before you start!

THE SEARCH FOR MJOLLNIR

Throw yourself into an action-packed Viking saga!

Thor, the god of thunder, has lost his hammer, and you must find it for him before the evil giants launch their attack. Do you have the skill and knowledge that it takes?

HEAVENS ABOVE

If you were a Viking god, which one would you be?

Find out with the help of this personality test. Answer the questions to discover whether you're more of a Frey than a Freyja.

HNEFATAFL

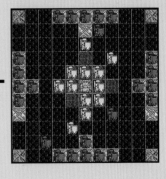

Give hnefatafl a try. It's the board game Vikings loved to play.

Find yourself an opponent, read the rules, then brave the board. By clicking your mouse, you can also find out more about the history of the game.

What's in the book

*All words in the text that appear in **bold** can be found in the glossary*

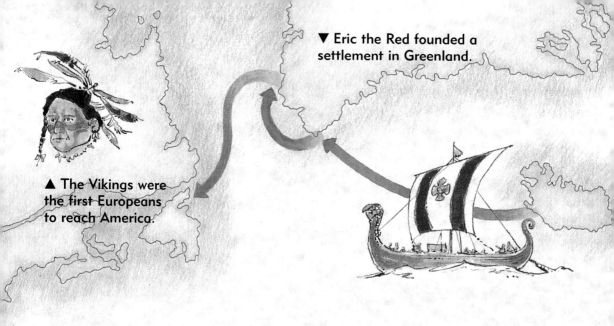

▼ Eric the Red founded a settlement in Greenland.

▲ The Vikings were the first Europeans to reach America.

"on 8 june the ravages of heathen men miserably destroyed God's church on Lindisfarne with plunder and slaughter..."

(ANGLO SAXON CHRONICLE. 793)

▶ The wealthy, unprotected monastery on the island of Lindisfarne was an easy target for the Vikings.

The Viking world

Many European people had their first glimpse of the Vikings when Viking **longships** appeared off their coasts. No one was prepared for the invading warriors, and few countries could resist the Vikings. From the first attacks in A.D. 787, Viking raids were a frequent occurrence all over northwestern Europe for the next 200 years.

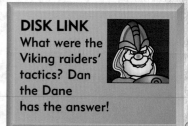

DISK LINK
What were the Viking raiders' tactics? Dan the Dane has the answer!

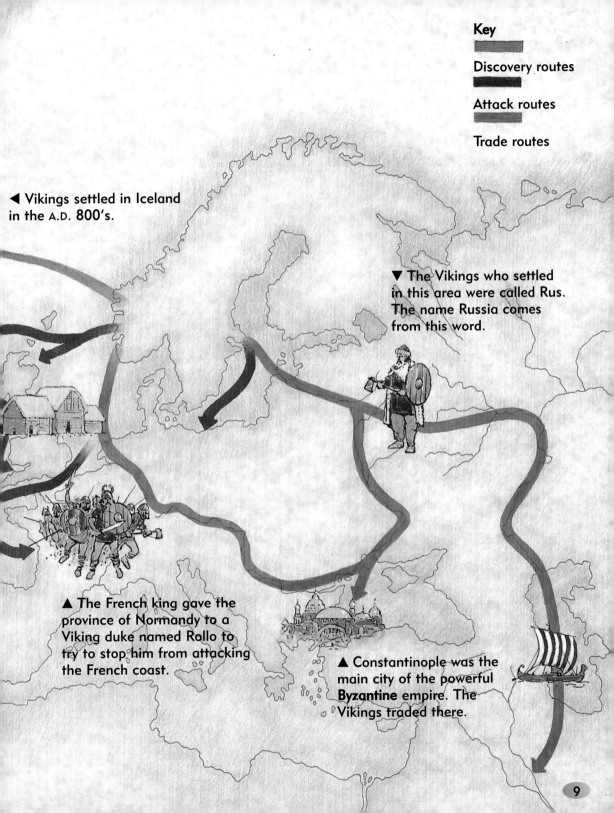

◀ Vikings settled in Iceland in the A.D. 800's.

▼ The Vikings who settled in this area were called Rus. The name Russia comes from this word.

▲ The French king gave the province of Normandy to a Viking duke named Rollo to try to stop him from attacking the French coast.

▲ Constantinople was the main city of the powerful **Byzantine** empire. The Vikings traded there.

9

Viking lands

Vikings came from the northern European countries that are now called Sweden, Norway, and Denmark. These lands are cold and bleak, with deep rivers, rocky coasts, and towering mountains. Even though the Vikings fished and hunted wild animals, there was not enough land to produce food for all of them.

Many Vikings sought a better life by using their skills as seafarers and warriors.

Viking lands were divided into several kingdoms. The richest, most powerful men became leaders such as kings and dukes. These leaders would call the **free men** to a meeting called the **Althing**, where they would discuss plans about expeditions to other countries or make decisions about local problems. Often, the kingdoms fought wars with one another, particularly over pieces of good land.

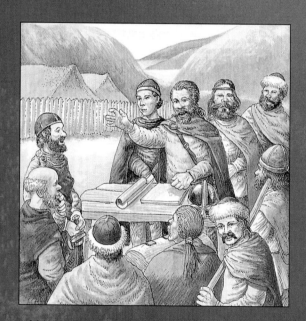

▲ Viking men gather for the Althing.

◄ The narrow, deep-watered fjords of Scandinavia form perfect natural harbors.

DISK LINK
Find out why Viking settlements were usually built on a fjord in Viking Village.

Pirates or traders?

Pirates

The Vikings attacked the lands around them, particularly England and France. They stole food and treasures and carried people away to make them slaves. People who lived in isolated areas on the coast or on islands were terrified of Viking attacks. Most of them were farmers and were not used to defending themselves and their families. They added to their daily prayers the words "God deliver us from the fury of the **Northmen**."

▼ Rope was wrapped around the **hilt** of Viking swords to make them easier to grip.

▲ Viking helmets like this one have been found at a number of gravesites in Europe. Soldiers were often buried with all their weapons because the Vikings believed they would need them in the afterlife.

Traders

In certain places, the Vikings got food and goods by trading rather than by attacking and stealing. This was usually when the inhabitants were stronger and could defend themselves. Vikings traveled as far as the Black Sea, trading their furs, jewelry, and slaves for spices and wine.

▶ Goods were sold for a weight, rather than a number, of gold or silver coins. When the Vikings needed change, they simply broke a coin in half!

DISK LINK
What was the most popular Viking weapon? Dan the Dane has the answer!

Longships

The Vikings were superb seafarers and used ships for traveling on the lakes, seas, and fjords of Scandinavia – as well as for trips farther away from home. Vikings measured their ships by their number of oars. The smallest, a faering, had four oars, and the largest, a longship, had about 32. The oars were used on inland waters when there wasn't enough wind to fill the sail.

A big longship could be up to 98 feet (30 meters) long and would travel up to 20 miles (32 kilometers) per hour under full sail. Ships were so important to the Vikings that their language contained dozens of different ways of saying "ship."

The Vikings could navigate by watching the stars and sun, as well as by using familiar landmarks such as islands and mountains. They also looked out for birds found in different places at different times of the year, such as puffins and fulmars.

▶ Vikings used oars when the sail was not up, when there was no wind, or when they sailed on inland waters. Each rower sat on a box, which held his belongings and a waterproof, reindeer-skin sleeping bag.

▶ The gaps between the oak planks of the ship were made waterproof by filling them with sheep's wool dipped in tar.

▲ Viking ships were among the first to have a **keel**. A keel keeps a ship stable, even in rough seas, and increases a ship's top speed in the water.

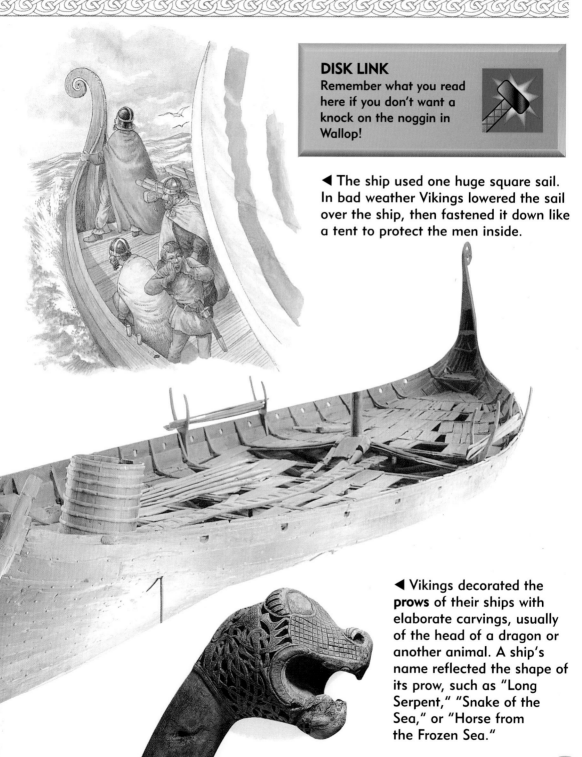

DISK LINK
Remember what you read here if you don't want a knock on the noggin in Wallop!

◀ The ship used one huge square sail. In bad weather Vikings lowered the sail over the ship, then fastened it down like a tent to protect the men inside.

◀ Vikings decorated the **prows** of their ships with elaborate carvings, usually of the head of a dragon or another animal. A ship's name reflected the shape of its prow, such as "Long Serpent," "Snake of the Sea," or "Horse from the Frozen Sea."

Heroes

The Vikings admired bold and fearless men, such as soldiers, sailors, and explorers. The deeds of these heroes were told so often that they became more like myths than historical fact.

DISK LINK
Can you guess how Vinland got its name? Dan the Dane will tell you!

Leif Ericson

The first people to sail from Europe to North America were Vikings! In 1002, Leif Ericson led an expedition to the coast of what is now the United States. The Vikings named the country Vinland and built a village there. Three years later, the Vikings were attacked by Native Americans and soon left.

King Cnut

In 1016, a Viking from Denmark named Cnut, son of the chieftain Sweyn Forkbeard, became king of England. He was a wise ruler who brought peace and stability.

Harald Haardraade

The Byzantine emperor used an elite Viking fighting force called the **Varangarian Guard**. Harald Haardraade, or Hard-nose, was a famous member. Later, as king of Norway, he was the last Viking to land with an army in England.

Sagas and runes

Viking children did not go to school. Instead, lessons came in the form of long stories, or sagas. Sagas described the adventures of the gods or of great Viking warriors. The stories were important ways of teaching history, geography, and navigation. The Vikings decorated some buildings with pictures from famous sagas.

▲ This wood carving shows Sigurd the Dragon-Slayer attacking a dragon.

▲ This stone carving shows one of the tales of Odin, the Vikings' god of war. You can see Odin in the center at the top, handing a sword to an old man.

The Futhark

The Viking alphabet was called the **futhark**. The letters, or **runes**, were made up mostly of straight lines and usually carved into wood or stone.

> **DISK LINK**
> Write your own message in runes and find out more about the futhark in Rune Writing.

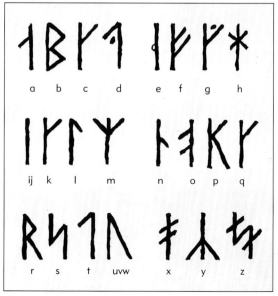

a b c d   e f g h

ij k l m   n o p q

r s t uvw   x y z

The Viking gods

The Vikings believed there were many different gods who lived in a place called **Asgard.** Each god was responsible for a different part of Viking life, such as war, travel, or the home. These gods were not perfect. They had human qualities and human weaknesses, such as jealousy and greed.

If a Viking died in battle, he was thought to go to a hall in Asgard called **Valhalla,** where everybody fought all day and feasted all night.

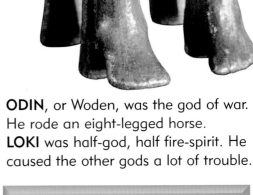

Thor

Some important gods

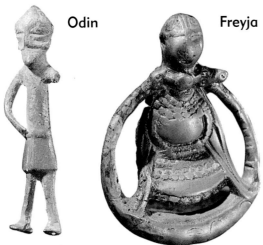

Odin   Freyja

THOR, the god of thunder, was the most popular god. He had a quick temper but was very good-hearted.

FREY made sure that the sun shined, the rain fell, and the crops grew. He kept his magic boat folded up in his pocket.

FREYJA was Frey's sister and the goddess of love. She could turn herself into a bird.

ODIN, or Woden, was the god of war. He rode an eight-legged horse.

LOKI was half-god, half fire-spirit. He caused the other gods a lot of trouble.

DISK LINK
Which Viking god are you most like? Find out in Heavens Above.

▲ When Viking warriors died, their bodies were often put in longships, which were then buried or set on fire and pushed out to sea.

▶ By the end of the Viking age, the Vikings were turning to Christianity. This mold from the A.D. 900's was used to make crosses and copies of Mjollnir, Thor's hammer.

At home

The Vikings were not only skilled soldiers and seafarers, but also farmers who lived with their families, growing and making everything they needed. Children helped as soon as they were able to. Even very small children had their own jobs, such as feeding the animals or gathering firewood.

Viking women worked on the farm and wove material for clothes and blankets on small looms. When their husbands were away fighting, they took care of the whole farm.

Viking houses were made of timber and woven branches, with turf or thatched roofs. Where wood was not available, Vikings built their homes out of stone. Inside, the houses were divided into rooms by stretching cloth or skins between the pillars that supported the roof.

A typical farm included the family house, or houses if the family was large. There were also sheds for the animals, a workshop for making metal tools, and small huts for slaves.

Hygiene

● Viking houses were not as clean as modern ones. Families left bones and vegetable scraps on the floor all winter and did not clear them out until spring.

● In spring, they buried garbage outside.

● Vikings often suffered from head lice, so most people had combs.

Games

Children had time to play games and carve wooden toys. In winter they made ice skates by carving bone blades and strapping them to their shoes with leather.

On dark, cold evenings, Viking children may have played a game called **hnefatafl,** which was similar to chess.

DISK LINK
Learn how to play hnefatafl on the disk and challenge a friend to a game.

Crafts

Vikings were very skilled craftworkers, making objects from stone, wood, and metal. Many of the most beautiful objects were made not by artists, but by ordinary people. A farmer might make a brooch using the same furnace he used to make his plow.

Because there were no banks, rich Vikings wore their wealth in the form of jewelry. This was the best way to keep it safe.

Blacksmiths were highly respected. Thor, one of the important Viking gods, used a smith's hammer as his main weapon.

▲ Some jewelry was made especially to be buried with a dead person. This arm-ring was found at a burial site.

Make Viking jewelry

Look at the decorations on the Viking objects in this book. Can you see how all the figures are woven around one another? The Vikings loved to use complicated patterns for decoration.

Try making a bracelet or brooch from modeling clay using Viking designs.

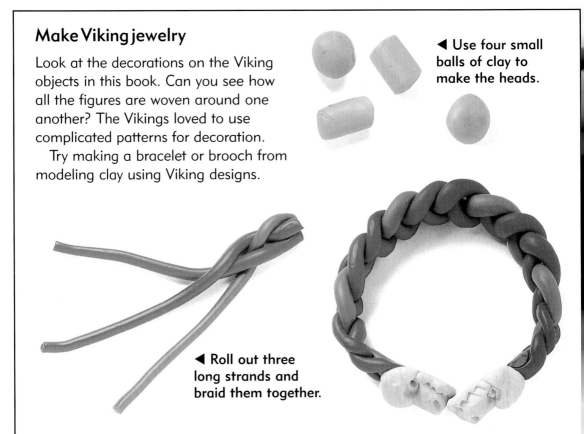

◀ Use four small balls of clay to make the heads.

◀ Roll out three long strands and braid them together.

▼ This mold was used to make part of a helmet. Once the mold was made, it could be used to decorate many helmets.

► This gold pendant was worn around the neck as a magical charm. Look at the elaborate patterns that cover it.

► The symbol of Thor's hammer was often used in jewelry. This silver hammer head is ornate, but many were simpler.

Food

Food was an important part of the Vikings' life. Very little land was fertile, and the winters were long and harsh. The Vikings ate fish and stews of beef or lamb. They grew vegetables such as peas, cabbage, beans, wild leeks, and garlic.

Tables were set up for meals, and family members would sit on the same wooden benches that they slept on at night. They ate from rectangular wooden platters or soapstone bowls, using spoons and knives that they carried on their belts.

The Vikings used drinking horns as well as cups. The horns did not have flat bottoms, so they were passed around the table until they were empty. A man who could empty a drinking horn in one turn was admired. The usual drink was mead, a sweet beer made from honey.

Food facts

● The Vikings used peas to make bread when they had no grain.
● They got salt by boiling sea water.
● The Vikings ate two meals a day: the day meal after the early farm work and the night meal at the end of the day.

DISK LINK
Feast your eyes on a typical Viking menu in the Viking Village.

▼ Vikings cooked over an open hearth fire. They roasted meat on huge spits and made stews in big iron caldrons. Sometimes they used a gridiron made of coiled iron, below. They heated it in a fire then placed it underneath a cooking pot. Does it remind you of part of a modern stove?

▼ Bowls were made from pottery

Clothes

Most Viking clothes were made from coarse woolen cloth, though some rich Vikings wore imported silk or linen. In winter, people wore furs to keep warm.

Men wore undershirts, breeches, long woolen trousers, and long tunics. Around their waists they wore a leather belt that carried purses, spoons, and knives.

Women wore wool or linen dresses with a tunic that looked like an apron attached with brooches.

▲ Vikings made shoes from leather or goatskin laced up with strips of leather.

Thor visits the land of the giants

This story is part of a Viking saga. It is about Thor, the god of thunder, and the journey he made to prove his strength. His journey and trials of strength would have been very familiar to the Vikings.

One summer day, Thor, Loki, and their two servants set off to visit Utgard, the land of the giants. After a long journey, they arrived at the gates of Utgard to find them locked. Thor hammered on the gates, calling for someone to come and let them in, but Loki slipped through the bars, dragging the others after him. They walked into the great hall of Utgard. In the middle was a long table around which hundreds of giants were seated on benches, eating and drinking. The giants all began to laugh as Thor marched up to the Giant King, who was seated at the far end of the hall.

"Greetings, Giant King," said Thor.

The king sat chewing bones and ignored Thor. From time to time he tossed a bone over his shoulder and picked up a new one.

Thor spoke again, this time a little louder: "Greetings, Gi – "

The Giant King interrupted: "So you're the great thunder god, Thor, are you? Well, you look awfully scrawny to me. I suppose you've come to test your strength?"

Thor was furious at the Giant King's rudeness, but he did not want to lose his temper when he was surrounded by giants.

"What skill would you like to challenge us with?" continued the Giant King.

Thor looked at the giants all around.

"I doubt if anyone here can drink as much as I can," Thor replied.

The Giant King signaled to a servant, who brought forward a huge drinking horn.

"This is used by my followers," he said. "A good drinker can finish it in one try. Let us see what the great Thor can do!"

Thor took the horn, raised it to his mouth and began to drink. He felt sure he could swallow it all, but he ran out of breath and found that it was no less full than before. He drank a second time, and this time the horn was no longer brimming full. He drank a third time, but although the level was lower than before, the horn was by no means empty.

"You don't seem to be much of a drinker," said the Giant King. "Why not try your strength? The younger giants like to test themselves by lifting my cat. We don't think this is much of a feat, but perhaps you'd like to try?"

Standing beside the Giant King's chair was the most enormous cat Thor had ever seen. Thor braced himself and then put both arms under the cat and heaved. The cat simply arched its back. Thor heaved again and managed to make the cat lift one paw off the ground before he had to admit defeat.

"As I thought," said the Giant King. "You may be strong in Asgard and in the realms of men, but your strength is nothing here."

Thor grew angry at this. "I can match any of your men in a fight. Just let anyone here wrestle with me."

There was a roar of laughter from all the giants in the hall.

"Everyone here feels that wrestling with you would be too easy," said the Giant King. "But, you could fight Elli, my foster mother."

A wrinkled old woman hobbled forward.

Thor thought that the Giant King was making fun of him until Elli took hold of him. Then he knew that his strength would be sorely tested. They struggled and fought, but eventually Elli threw Thor off balance and he landed on one knee.

"Enough, enough!" shouted the Giant King. "You have also shown us that you are no wrestler either. You pose no threat, so you may eat with us and spend the night here."

Thor and his companions were hungry and tired after their long journey. When they had eaten, they spread their bedding in a space on the floor among the giants.

Thor awoke early, before any of the giants, and roused his companions.

"Come, let's go before the giants wake up," he whispered.

They tiptoed over the sleeping giants and out of the gates of Utgard. To their surprise, they found the Giant King already outside waiting for them. He walked with them across the plain for a while. He finally stopped and said: "This is where I must leave you. Thor, do not feel upset about your failures last night."

Thor was puzzled. "But I have never before been so badly beaten," he said.

The Giant King replied: "You were not competing in a fair fight. I feared your strength, so I used magic to deceive you. The other end of the horn that you drank from was in the sea. When you reach the shore, you will see just how much you have lowered its level. The cat you lifted was really the giant serpent whose body is wrapped around the world. You managed to lift it until its back touched the sky. And as for Elli, it was a wonder you withstood her for so long. You see, Elli is Old Age, which defeats all men in time."

Thor was furious. He seized his hammer and swung it around, but the Giant King and Utgard had vanished, as if they had never been there at all.

DISK LINK
Throw yourself into a thrilling interactive saga. Try playing The Search for Mjollnir if you dare!

How we know

Have you ever wondered how we know so much about the Vikings' lives, even though they lived more than 1,000 years ago?

Evidence from the ground

Many ordinary objects, which were thrown away by the Vikings when they were no longer needed, have been found preserved.

Some important Vikings were buried in ships that were full of their possessions. Archaeologists gain valuable information about the Vikings when these ships are discovered.

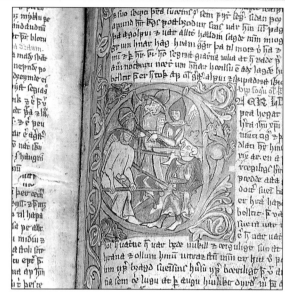

Evidence around us

Many places in Europe originally had Viking names, so we can tell where the Vikings settled.

In France, Normandy – meaning "land of the Northmen" – was ruled by the Vikings.

Many British place names have the Viking endings *-thorpe* and *-by*, like Scunthorpe and Grimsby.

Also, Wednesday was originally Woden's day, and Thursday was Thor's day.

Evidence from books

Many of the stories told by the Vikings were written down, and so it is very easy to find out who the important gods were and what various historical figures did. We even know that when Eric the Red discovered Greenland, he gave it that name in spite of its cold iciness because "many would want to go there if it had so promising a name."

Glossary

The **Althing** was a council of free men that met when problems arose. This was the Vikings' only form of government.

The Vikings believed that **Asgard** was where their gods lived, and where they themselves would go when they died.

The **Byzantine** empire in the East was the strongest world power at the time of the Vikings. It lasted from the A.D. 500's to the 1400's.

The **day meal** was the first meal of the day. It was eaten after the early farm work had been done.

Free men were all the men who were not slaves. Slaves were usually people who had been captured on raids.

The smallest type of Viking ship was a **faering**. It had four oars.

The **Futhark** was the runic alphabet used by the Vikings. The word is taken from the sound of the first six letters.

A **gridiron** was a coiled metal strip that was placed in the fire and used to heat pots.

Hnefatafl was a board game played by the Vikings.

A **keel** is the long timber that forms the lowest part of a ship and helps it to balance.

A **longship** was the long, low ship used by the Vikings. Longship is also the secret password to get Roland to reveal the Vikings' military secrets in Ask Roland.

Mjollnir was Thor's hammer. He carried it with him at all times.

The **night meal** was the meal eaten after all the work was done, when it began to grow dark.

Northmen was the name given to the Vikings by the people they attacked or traded with. "Viking" was a term they used to describe themselves.

The **prow** is the front end of a ship.

A **rune** is a letter of the Viking alphabet. Runes were made up of straight lines because they were intended to be carved in wood or stone.

A **saga** is an adventure story of gods or heroes. Although sagas were usually passed on by word of mouth, some were written down.

Scandinavia is the group of countries from which the Vikings originated. They include Denmark, Norway, Sweden, and Iceland.

Valhalla is the hall in Asgard where warriors hoped to go when they died. Here they could fight all day and feast all night.

The **Varangarian Guard** was a section of the Byzantine army made up of Vikings. The Varangarian Guard was the emperor's bodyguard.

Lab pages

Photocopy these sheets and use them to make your own notes.

Rules of hnefatafl

Hnefatafl was one of the Vikings' favorite games. It is a two-player game, similar to chess – so you'll need someone to play against. The rules are very easy to learn. The idea of the game is based on a Viking raid.

- There are two armies – attackers and defenders.

- The attacking army's pieces are blue, and the defender's pieces are white.

- The attacker's army tries to trap the king so that he cannot move.

- Once the king is trapped, the attackers have won and the game is over.

- The defender's army tries to help the king escape to safety.

- To win the game, the defender's king must get to one of the green squares at any of the four corners.

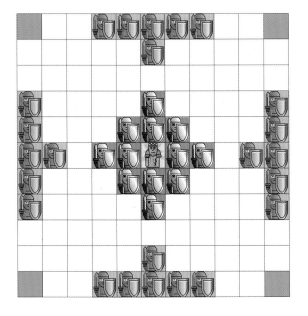

▲ At the start of the game, the king is on the central square, surrounded by his white defending army. The attacking army is lined up along the four edges of the board.

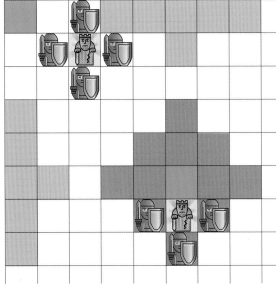

▲ The attacking army's pieces can trap and capture the king by surrounding him on all four sides or on just three sides against the central square.

- Players take turns, moving one piece at a time.

- All the pieces on the board move in exactly the same way.

- All the pieces move in straight lines – up and down or from side to side.

- You can move a piece as many squares as you like. But you are not allowed to jump other pieces.

- Pieces are not allowed to land on a square that is already occupied by another piece.

- All pieces can jump across the square in the middle as long as the king isn't on it!

- The king's squares are the central square and the green ones in each corner. Only the king can land on one of the king's squares.

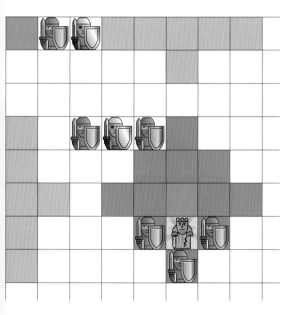

▲ Any piece can be captured when trapped between two of its opponent's pieces or between one of the corner squares and an opponent's piece.

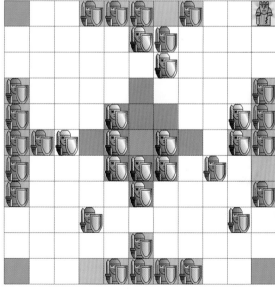

▲ Finally, the defender's king wins the game by avoiding captivity and landing on one of the green squares at any of the four corners of the board.

Loading your INTERFACT disk

INTERFACT is easy to load. But, before you begin, quickly run through the checklist on the opposite page to ensure that your computer is ready to run the program.

Your INTERFACT CD-ROM will run on both PCs with Windows and on Apple Macs. To make sure that your computer meets the system requirements, check the list below.

SYSTEM REQUIREMENTS

PC/WINDOWS
- Pentium 100Mhz processor
- Windows 95 or 98 (or later)
- 16Mb RAM (24Mb recommended for Windows 98)
- VGA 256 color monitor
- SoundBlaster-compatible soundcard
- 1Mb graphics card
- Double-speed CD-ROM drive

APPLE MAC
- 68020 processor (PowerMac or G3/iMac recommended)
- System 7.0 (or later)
- 16Mb RAM
- Color monitor set to at least 480 x 640 pixels and 256 colors
- Double-speed CD-ROM drive

LOADING INSTRUCTIONS

You can run INTERFACT from the CD – you don't need to install it on your hard drive.

PC WITH WINDOWS 95 OR 98

The program should start automatically when you put the disk in the CD drive. If it does not, follow these instructions.

1. Put the disk in the CD drive
2. Open MY COMPUTER
3. Double-click on the CD drive icon
4. Double-click on the icon called VIKINGS

PC WITH WINDOWS 3.1 OR 3.11

1. Put the disk in the CD drive
2. Select RUN from the FILE menu in the PROGRAM MANAGER
3. Type D:\VIKINGS (Where D is the letter of your CD drive)
4. Press the RETURN key

APPLE MAC

1. Put the disk in the CD drive
2. Double-click on the INTERFACT icon
3. Double-click on the icon called VIKINGS

CHECKLIST

● Firstly, make sure that your computer and monitor meet the system requirements as set out on page 40.

● Ensure that your computer, monitor and CD-ROM drive are all switched on and working normally.

● It is important that you do not have any other applications, such as wordprocessors, running. Before starting INTERFACT quit all other applications.

● Make sure that any screen savers have been switched off.

● If you are running INTERFACT on a PC with Windows 3.1 or 3.11, make sure that you type in the correct instructions when loading the disk, using a colon (:) not a semi-colon (;) and a back slash (\) not a forward slash (/). Also, do not use any other punctuation or put any spaces between letters.

41

How to use INTERFACT

INTERFACT is easy to use.
First find out how to run the program
(see page 40), then read these simple
instructions and dive in!

You will find that there are lots of different features to explore.
Choose the feature you want to play using the controls on the right-hand side of the screen. You will see that the main area of the screen changes as you click on different features.

For example, this is what your screen will look like when you choose to explore Viking Village, where you can learn all about how the Vikings lived. Once you've selected a feature, click on the main screen to start playing.

These Vikings are having a meal. To find out more about the Vikings' eating habits click here

Click to continue

Click here to select the feature you would like to explore.

Click on the arrow keys to scroll through the different features on the disk or find your way to the exit.

This is the text box where instructions and directions appear. Go to page 4 to find out what's on the disk.

DISK LINKS

When you read the book, you'll come across Disk Links. These show you where to find activities on the disk that relate to the page you are reading. Use the arrow keys to find the icon on screen that matches the one in the Disk Link.

DISK LINK
Would you like to play a Viking board game? Try hnefatafl!

BOOKMARKS

As you explore the features on the disk, you'll see Bookmarks. These show you where to look in the book for more information about the topic on screen. Just turn to the page of the book shown in the Bookmark.

23

LAB PAGES

On pages 36 - 37 you'll find note pages for you to photocopy. These are for making notes and recording any feelings or ideas you may have about what you've read.

HOT DISK TIPS

- After you have chosen the feature you want to play, remember to move the cursor from the icon to the main screen before clicking on the mouse again.

- If you don't know how to use one of the on-screen controls, simply touch it with your cursor. An explanation will pop up in the text box!

- Keep a close eye on the cursor. When it changes from an arrow ➔ to a hand, ☞ click your mouse and something will happen.

- Any words that appear on screen in blue and underlined are "hot." This means you can touch them with the cursor for more information.

- Explore the screen! There are secret hot spots and hidden surprises to find.

Troubleshooting

If you come across a problem loading or running the INTERFACT disk, you should find the solution here. If you still cannot solve your problem, call the helpline at 1-800-424-1280.

QUICK FIXES   Run through these general checkpoints before consulting COMMON PROBLEMS on the next page.

QUICK FIXES   PC WITH WINDOWS 3.1 OR 3.11

1 Check that you have the minimum system requirements: 386/33Mhz, VGA color monitor, 4Mb of RAM.

2 Make sure you have typed in the correct instructions: a colon (:) not a semi-colon (;) and a back slash (\) not a forward slash (/). Also, do not put any spaces between letters or punctuation.

3 It is important that no other applications are running. Before you start **INTERFACT**, hold down the Control key and press Escape. If you find that other programs are open, click on them with the mouse, then click the End Task key.

QUICK FIXES   PC WITH WINDOWS 95

1 Make sure you have typed in the correct instructions: a colon (:) not a semi-colon (;) and a back slash(\) not a forward slash (/). Also, do not put any spaces between letters or punctuation.

2 Make sure no other applications are running. Before you start **INTERFACT**, look at the task bar. If other applications are open, click with the right mouse button and select Close from the pop-up menu.

MACINTOSH

1 Make sure that you have the minimum system requirements: 68020 processor, 640x480 color display, system 7.0 (or a later version) and 4Mb of RAM.

2 Make sure no other programs are running. Before you start **INTERFACT**, click the application menu in the top right corner. Select each of the open applications and select Quit from the File menu.

COMMON PROBLEMS

Symptom: Cannot load disk.
Problem: There is not enough space available on your hard disk.
Solution: Make more space available by deleting old applications and files you don't use until 6Mb of free space is available.

Symptom: Disk will not run.
Problem: There is not enough memory available.
Solution: *Either* quit other open applications (see Quick Fixes) *or* increase your machine's RAM by adjusting the Virtual Memory.

Symptom: Graphics do not load or are poor quality.
Problem: *Either* there is not enough memory available *or* you have the wrong display setting.
Solution: *Either* quit other applications (see Quick Fixes) *or* make sure that your monitor control is set to 640x480x256 or VGA.

Symptom: There is no sound (PCs only).
Problem: Your sound card is not Soundblaster compatible.
Solution: Try to configure your sound settings to make them Soundblaster compatible (refer to your sound card manual for more details).

Symptom: Your machine freezes.
Problem: There is not enough memory available.
Solution: *Either* quit other applications (see Quick Fixes) *or* increase your machine's RAM by adjusting the Virtual Memory.

Symptom: Text does not fit neatly into boxes and "hot" copy does not bring up extra information.
Problem: Standard fonts on your computer have been moved or deleted.
Solution: Reinstall standard fonts. The PC version requires Arial; the Macintosh version requires Helvetica. See your computer manual for further information.

Index